A VINDICATION OF POLITICAL VIRTUE

A
VINDICATION
OF
POLITICAL
VIRTUE

THE POLITICAL THEORY OF

MARY WOLLSTONECRAFT

VIRGINIA SAPIRO

THE UNIVERSITY OF CHICAGO PRESS
Chicago & London

VIRGINIA SAPIRO is professor of political science and of women's studies at the University of Wisconsin.

The University of Chicago Press, Chicago 60637
The University of Chicago Press, Ltd., London
© 1992 by The University of Chicago
All rights reserved. Published 1992
Printed in the United States of America
01 00 99 98 97 96 95 94 93 92   5 4 3 2 1

ISBN (cloth): 0-226-73490-0
ISBN (paper): 0-226-73491-9

Library of Congress Cataloging-in-Publication Data

Sapiro, Virginia.
    A vindication of political virtue : the political theory of Mary
Wollstonecraft / Virginia Sapiro.
        p.   cm.
    Includes bibliographical references (p.   ) and index.
    1. Wollstonecraft, Mary, 1759–1797—Contributions in political
science.   2. Wollstonecraft, Mary, 1759–1797—Contributions in
feminism.   3. Wollstonecraft, Mary, 1759–1797—Contributions in
women's rights.   I. Title.
JC176.W65S27   1992
323.3′4′092—dc20   91-38426

TO

GRAHAM

BECAUSE HE PROVES THAT EVEN
MW WASN'T ALWAYS RIGHT

*But one grand truth women have yet to learn, though much it imports them
to act accordingly. In the choice of a husband, they should not be
led astray by the qualities of a lover—for a lover the husband, even
supposing him to be wise and virtuous, cannot long remain.*

A Vindication of the Rights of Woman

CONTENTS

ADVERTISEMENT

In many works of this species, the hero is allowed to be mortal, and to become wise and virtuous as well as happy, by a train of events and circumstances. The heroines, on the contrary, are to be born immaculate; and to act like goddesses of wisdom, just come forth highly finished Minervas from the head of Jove.

(Wrongs, 83)

n an era in which the Author has been disappeared, or at least held hostage by theories allowing definition only by the Reader, it is perhaps presumptuous for an author to reveal who appears in her mind as readers, and what problems those appearances present to her writing. But it is necessary, and the eighteenth-century custom of addressing the (gentle) reader, person to person, is worth reviving.

This text is marked by the writer's simultaneous experience in different intellectual communities. I am a political scientist; my approach to theory is unmistakably grounded in the practices and canon of that field. I am also a member of the interdisciplinary field of women's studies, therefore my approach has been reshaped by what I have learned from theorists grounded in literary studies and history. In addition, most of my previous work has been in the "empirical" mode, and my method here will show signs of this as well.

In this book I address audiences I believe to have some distinctly different interests, perspectives, standards of evaluation, and even languages, although they overlap at many points, one of which is that they all have things to learn from Mary Wollstonecraft. Political theorists will find more literary analysis than they are used to seeing; other feminist theorists may not like my use of such theory and may find it "inexpert." The interests that drove me to political science and keep me there have made me less amenable to seduction by deconstruction than has widely been the case in feminist theory, but my acquaintance with it has been important. Feminist theorists from outside political philosophy may find I keep too much company with the old boys of that discipline. Political theorists from outside feminist studies may find my definition of "political" too broad, and may miss some familiar names among the notes while encountering too many unrecognizable ones.

I pursue arguments with different bodies of writing through my discussion of Mary Wollstonecraft and her work. Some of these writings were generated by feminist theorists, others by nonfeminist political theorists, some by theorists of particular flavors. I have tried to use a common enough language to allow as many as possible to participate in the whole, regardless of where they started.

This is neither a biography nor a straightforward explication of Wollstonecraft's writing. It is an attempt to pursue the paths to which she pointed. For that I must certainly begin with her life and work, but then always move away even while looking back.

ABBREVIATIONS

eferences to Wollstonecraft's writing are noted in the text. With the exception of her personal letters, all page numbers refer to the *Works of Mary Wollstonecraft*, edited by Marilyn Butler and Janet Todd. Page numbers for her letters refer to *The Collected Letters of Mary Wollstonecraft*, edited by Ralph Wardle. In the case of letters I have included the date of writing and for book reviews the date of publication in the reference. Following is a list of abbreviations used.

"Cave": "The Cave of Fancy," a fragment, 1798.

Elements: Translation of Christian Salzmann, *Elements Of Morality*, 1790.

FrRev: An Historical and Moral View of the Origin and Progress of the French Revolution, 1794.

Grandison: Translation of Maria de Cambon, *Young Grandison*, 1790.

"Hints": "Hints," 1798.

"Let. French": "Letter on the Present Character of the French Nation," 1798.

Letters: Personal correspondence.

"Management": "Fragment of Letters on the Management of Infants," 1797.

"Poetry": "On Poetry, and Our Relish of the Beauties of Nature," 1797.

Mary: Mary: A Fiction, 1788.

Reader: The Female Reader, 1789.

Religious: Translation of Jacques Necker, *Of the Importance of Religious Opinions*, 1788.

Revs: Reviews published in the *Analytical Review*, 1788–1797.

Scand.: Letters Written during a Short Residence in Sweden, Norway, and Denmark. 1796.

Stories: Original Stories from Real Life, 1788.

Thoughts: Thoughts on the Education of Daughters, 1787.

VM: A Vindication of the Rights of Men, 1790.

VW: A Vindication of the Rights of Woman, 1792.

Wrongs: The Wrongs of Woman, or Maria, 1798.

PREFACE

I do not approve of your preface. . . . If your work should deserve attention it is a blur on the very face of it.—Disadvantages of education &c ought, in my opinion, never to be pleaded [with the public] in excuse for defects of any importance, because if the writer has not sufficient strength of mind to overcome the common difficulties which lie in his way, nature seems to command him, with a very audible voice, to leave the task of instructing others to those who can. This kind of vain humility has ever disgusted me—and I should say to an author, who humbly sued for forbearance, 'if you have not a tolerably good opinion of your own production, why intrude it on the public? We have plenty of bad books already. . . .' (Letters 1792:219)[1]*

he fourth quarter of centuries has recently (in century terms) taken on great significance for students and practitioners of democratic theory and politics. Twentieth-century celebratory commissions engaged in almost maniacal organizational efforts for the anniversaries of 1776, 1788, and 1789, among others, although 1688 was almost ignored for a variety of reasons. Depending on the further history of Eastern Europe and the USSR, 1989–90 may provide another Important Date for future celebrations.

Such commemorations serve many functions. They are certainly good for tourist industries. They are national and nationalistic solidarity rituals. But they also focus our attention, at least briefly, to reconsider the histories we take for granted. Perhaps the period costumes and reproductions force some of us to reflect on the enormity and human significance of what are otherwise set texts and events. They may make us ask where we would have been and what we would have done if we had been alive at such times.

A related date indirectly forced my hand to this text: 1792. That year, thirty-two-year-old Mary Wollstonecraft published *A Vindication of the Rights of Woman,* a pamphlet often hailed—or decried—as the first major work of feminist political theory. This work appeared in the midst of a writing career that began in the late 1780s with a novel, works on education, and a Grub Street career of translations and reviews. She became, as she put it, "the first of a new genus": a woman supporting herself by writing. Her career ended in 1797, when she died as a result of childbirth while the leaves of an unfinished novel lay on her desk.

The two-hundredth anniversary of the publication of *The Rights of Woman* should not be marked as the bicentennial of the birth of feminism.[2*] It is not strictly correct even to call Wollstonecraft a feminist. There was no such social movement in her time. She didn't invent the fact or idea and it is not even possible to argue that her work directly inspired anyone else to do so. Nevertheless, her writings and life story are essential elements in the history of feminism. Trying to understand the significance of her work after the passage of two centuries is a difficult task. Wollstonecraft's work has been explored in the context of the history of feminism and women's writing, but it must also be defined in relation to the history of political theory. She was a political theorist, even if most canonical theorists have not been taught to think so.[3*]

If memorial celebrations offer a chance to think of what was and what might have been, the possibilities suggested by Wollstonecraft's work are enormous. She offered a means for the liberal tradition, especially the more radical wing of it, to absorb women as well as men into its conception of citizens and citizenship. Anyone who knows anything about Wollstonecraft knows this about her. But she offered more: A means of stretching the liberal temperament to incorporate into political thinking explicit concern for the quality of the personal relations and day-to-day conditions of the lives of citizens. It is no wonder that Owenites, including Robert Owen himself, were fond of her, or that the anarchist Emma Goldman wrote of Wollstonecraft as though the older woman was a mirror in which the younger could scrutinize herself. But women were not integrated into liberal theory, radical or not, and political theory remained "about" what happens outside of families, households, and personal relationships.

We can read Wollstonecraft in relation to what is now regarded as our canonical past in order to understand both the traditions of political thinking that probed the connections between gender and politics and those that refused to do so or rested on unexamined assumptions about the nature of male and female. Indeed, only in the twentieth century did canonical political theory exclude explicit treatment of gender from political theory and argument.[4]* Earlier, gender had been included at least to argue for (and occasionally against) the subjection of women. In this century it has been said (incorrectly) that political argument has been essentially gender-neutral and therefore posed no special problems for women. Recently perhaps, political theorists have been more aware that they speak in mixed company. Questions relating to dominance and subordination on the basis of gender become a bit touchier under these circumstances.

Carefully marking one's text with the historical circumstances under which it was written is not the done thing in academic circles. One is supposed to appeal to the times, but books are usually expected to read as though they were written this morning. Nevertheless, it is important to "date" this book. A critical part of my purpose is to interrogate the problem of canons and theoretical and political traditions. This discussion cannot take place without attending to time and place. The texts I discuss have not been handed down from generation to generation and master to student; their history is very different. The more conventional history of canonical texts is no excuse for ignoring *their* history, but with my self-confessed intention of affecting tradition (and therefore history, at least as far as my successors would be concerned), it would be neglectful not to mark my time as well as Wollstonecraft's.

The work of earlier Wollstonecraft interpreters is clearly marked by the influence of their times. Those clustering at the beginning of the century often paint Wollstonecraft as the first of a line of feminists leading through the suffrage movements of the United States and Great Britain to the eventual victory. Not surprisingly, most Wollstonecraft interpreters of that period regarded this direction as a victory. The new women's movement, its issues, organization, and controversies, served as the backdrop of a much larger collection of later Wollstonecraft biographies.[5]* With few exceptions, the state of the women's movement shaped the way Wollstonecraft's story was told.

The end of the twentieth century is a time of political reassessment and historical reflection. The recent commemorations of revolutions, the new or at least apparent revolutions in some places and the attempts elsewhere have undoubtedly influenced my reading of Wollstonecraft. Certainly I was led to take special account of the centrality of the French Revolution in Wollstonecraft's life and writings. Her first political disquisition, *A Vindication of the Rights of Men*, was one of the earliest of the answers to Edmund Burke's *Reflections on the French Revolution*. At the end of 1792, nearly a year after she completed *A Vindication of the*

Rights of Woman, she left for Paris and its environs. Her stay there coincided with the duration of the Terror.

The overtones of history were most forceful as I reread Wollstonecraft's 1794 work, *An Historical and Moral View of the French Revolution.* Here was Wollstonecraft the political idealist who believed in the ultimate possibility of enlightenment and the triumph of virtue in politics; who thought that the great liberal thinkers had shown the way. Like Richard Price and Joseph Priestley, she thought the French Revolution was at least the herald. But her book as well as contemporaneous letters she wrote reveal her loathing for the tyranny that had evolved within the Revolution. What did the idealistic political theorist write when she returned to her house, having had to cross streets red with blood? How does the political idealist confront political reality?[6]

I occasionally turned from reading this work to listening to the latest news from Eastern Europe. As tyrants go, Louis XVI and Marie Antoinette did not hold a candle to Nikolai and Elena Ceausescu. But as the Bourbons and Ceausescus fell at the same moment in my time, one family by guillotine, the other by firing squad, it would have been strange had the political questions these events raised not become entangled.

Partly because of the influence of intellectual movements such as women's studies, the scholarly world has recently experienced the more gentle, although not always pleasant, process of reassessing canons and intellectual traditions. Self-reflection leads, in turn, to reassessing the conventions of women's studies, short though the life of this movement has been. As much as this book was planned to be about Mary Wollstonecraft's political theory, her life and work became a vehicle for rethinking some old orthodoxies of political theory and some new orthodoxies of feminist theory. These are discussed most explicitly in the final two chapters.

Tratteggio

Anyone venturing into the study of a historical political theorist must be painfully aware of some of the continuing controversies surrounding the practice of political theory. I will forego the pleasures of entering the fray with extended discussion of general debates over history, recreation and interpretation, meaning and context, and all that is related. I have little new to add, and I wish to spend my energy and space on Wollstonecraft.[7] I will not avoid the controversies but simply make my choices and allow the critics to fall where they may—they will do so anyway.[8]

Graphic images may help illustrate one's orientation to the past. Lillian Hellman, for example, named a volume of her memoirs *Pentimento*.[9] She explained that *pentimento*, the image of earlier underlying paintings that emerge on a reused canvas, was an apt metaphor for her understanding of her autobiographical experience. She could not see even her own past directly but imagined it filtered through her present.

I have found a different term from the graphic arts useful in trying to describe my efforts in looking back to Mary Wollstonecraft: *tratteggio*. Tratteggio is a technique developed for conservation of wall paintings, used where portions of a picture have been destroyed. This is a complex and delicate process of making tiny parallel brush strokes that give the impression of filling in the missing parts when one stands back from it. In contrast to the older view that the object is to make the original and the retouched portions indistinguishable, as though the modern interpretation could be an accurate representation of the original, tratteggio grew out of the argument that although at a distance the composition should be rendered whole, the differentiation between original and retouching should be clearly maintained for closer inspection.

It is undeniably naive to believe one can reconstruct the entire authorial meaning of a text, especially if the author and everyone else from the time have long since died. Such reconstruction is probably an inappropriate task for a historical political theorist in any case. Nevertheless it is almost impossible—and probably absurd—to probe the meaning of texts without trying to understand something about what people were thinking and doing when they wrote them. One must do—and claim to do—something in between, something like a written version of tratteggio.

The more I worked with Wollstonecraft's texts and with works about her, the more I sensed a violence that has been done not just to her but to many others as well. These people and texts have been abstracted into passive signs. Perhaps due to working many years as a student of political behavior or, more likely, because I spent too much time gazing into my subjects' faces in the National Portrait Gallery, I could not forget that writing is an act of speech, and participation in political argument is a political activity, especially for those involved in oppositional politics. Wollstonecraft made many dangerous choices as personal and political acts; among them was writing the texts she has left us.

It will be obvious throughout that I find it necessary to ground writing and reading in both individual and societal history (or, more conventionally, biography and history) in order to interpret either. My interpretation of Wollstonecraft's texts is always shaped in part by imagining the social acts of reading and writing in the context of tangible lives. In this case the tangible life is that of a lower-middle-class Englishwoman with little formal education, who lived through the last half of the eighteenth century and survived by her pen during the period of the French Revolution. Indeed, she chose to witness that revolution firsthand. She identified herself with Dissenters at a time when being a member of the established church still accorded citizenship rights and privileges and with political radicals during a wave of conservative reaction. She was a woman who wrote political tracts, including two (counting her final novel) in vehement defense of women at a time when women had virtually no citizenship rights or privileges. She insisted on earning her own living from the time she was an adolescent and remained unmarried by choice until half-way through her second pregnancy.

I have tried to be particularly attentive to historical shifts in common meanings of key words and to the importance of social context in understanding those words. In a sense, one of the purposes of the early chapters is to develop a Wollstonecraft lexicon. Many terms that play important roles in Wollstonecraft's texts have undergone substantial changes in the way they are generally understood. Some were changing in her day. Some, such as *Gothic*, had a political buzz in her day that we no longer hear. The point is not just that we might be misguided by reading some words anachronistically, although this is the case. It is also true that words take on different meanings depending on who is speaking or of whom one is speaking. The fact that Wollstonecraft was a woman often speaking of women pushes us toward certain interpretations of words such as *virtue* or *sensibility* rather than others; that "push" may be misdirected.

One subject of politics is the creation and control of value, and one means to that end is the control of language. Conceptual change must be understood as an important part of the history of political change.[10] Wollstonecraft used a number of concepts that were contested in her day, such as *enthusiasm* and *sensibility*. She was clearly a participant in struggles over some of these concepts. This was most surely the case in her attempt to redefine *reason* and *virtue* with ungendered meaning.

I include some features of everyday life needed to understand the reference points of the text because such details of women's lives are not yet well incorporated into standard historical knowledge, even of highly educated people. It is necessary to know that when a late eighteenth-century woman talked about sexuality she herself was probably unable to prevent conception reliably if she engaged in sexual intercourse; that even if she were reasonably well off there was a strong possibility she would die as a result of pregnancy or childbirth. No doubt she would have been aware of the odds in the first case and probably aware of them in the second. Sexuality was—materially and not just conceptually—a life-and-death matter for women, as Wollstonecraft's own life demonstrates. It is difficult to imagine how one could seriously attempt interpretation of her writing on related matters without understanding these basic facts of life.

Wollstonecraft in Partisan Company

Someone has suggested that life would become easier for academics at conventions if they would wear tags indicating not their own name but the name of their favorite theorist or school of thought.[11]* Of course, footnotes serve in part as condensation symbols or partisan banners indicating association and membership, providing clues about intellectual and political temperament and often other more personal information such as whom one does and doesn't like. But these labels tell us less about the bearer than many people think.

Theorists concerned with democratic theory have been engaged in a number of overlapping arguments over appropriate identification of theory and theorists, especially in the eighteenth century. Central to the controversy are those who define much of the most important political argument in eighteenth-century England and America as a renaissance of the Renaissance, in which the challengers to the patriarchal and monarchical authority returned to civic humanism and classical republicanism for their fundamental principles.

This argument, identified most widely with J. G. A. Pocock, is itself a challenge to the earlier conventional argument that placed John Locke as the turning point in political thinking, apparently defining the development of democratic theory as a straight line forward from Locke, the ideological founding father. Those who have pursued the republicanism thesis are a diverse lot, including the "communitarians" who are intent on reminding us that possessive individualism is not the only heritage of liberal democratic theory. Against the new conventional view stands those who maintain that the brand of liberalism usually associated with Locke was, in fact, powerful at the end of the eighteenth century and after.[12]

My aim is not to resolve the controversy, although this book is, among other things, a contribution to it. The question I pose is considerably more narrow: What species of political theorist was Mary Wollstonecraft? Here Wollstonecraft interpreters imply different answers. Few have given her stance in relation to wider eighteenth-century political debates much attention because she, like many women who write about women, has often been treated as part of a segregated phenomenon. She has been read in light of other arguments about women but has been less often considered as a participant in the wider flow of political argument.

Where Wollstonecraft is identified in relation to the debates recognizable to students of political theory she is usually described by the generic term *liberal*. Her attachment to the language of the Enlightenment tradition and the titles of her two best-known pamphlets, *A Vindication of the Rights of Men* and *A Vindication of the Rights of Woman,* lead many to understand her work in terms of a stereotypical construction of Lockean liberalism based primarily in juridical rights, contracts, and individualism. Few have remarked on the contradiction between this conception and the circumstances of her intellectual life. Her favorite author (and also one of her two favorite foes) seems to have been Jean-Jacques Rousseau. She found her personal, intellectual, and political companionship in the radical Dissenting circle of London, most of whose members were among the minority of English supporters of the French Revolution. Her mentors were Richard Price and Joseph Priestley; among her friends were Tom Paine, Joseph Johnson, Ruth and Joel Barlow, Thomas Holcroft, Henri Fuseli, and William Godwin. This does not bode well for a Lockean interpretation of Mary Wollstonecraft.

Guilt by association is not a sufficient method of characterizing a theorist. But as I shall emphasize, her works from the 1790s are at least as infused with a language of republicanism as of legal rights. She was very serious about rights—as political writers without many rights must be—and her radicalism is grounded in Lockean terms in much the way Kramnick describes bourgeois radicals.[13] In her writings, the moral, social, and political world is also organized around a struggle between the forces of virtue and corruption. Those who make Wollstonecraft sound like a late eighteenth-century John Locke in drag mistake her. But she is also not a backward-looking seeker of a lost golden age. She was forthright in her contempt for Rousseau's "golden age of stupidity" (*Scand.* 288). She was one of many political writers of her day who would have been confused by the notion that one must be Lockean or republican but not both.

Wollstonecraft's writing also offers a severe test to posers of another dichotomy. Our modern intellectual heritage often seems anchored by two overdrawn figures. On one side is the rationalist Enlightenment thinker who emphasizes reason and mind to the exclusion of emotion, passion, and body. On the other side is the romantic who intuits the mysteries of the world through the senses and passions, and who knows that the intelligence of reason is only illusory. Wollstonecraft has often been accused of being one of the former, sometimes to an almost pathological point. Others, especially those who recognize the romanticism of her *Short Residence* and the profound influence of this work on romantic writers, including Coleridge and Wordsworth, see a "late Wollstonecraft" romantic, perhaps owing to a personality change that some attribute to her apparent release from reason by her lover Gilbert Imlay.

I shall pursue a different possibility. Although Wollstonecraft no doubt experienced some change in her thinking, reason and passion seem much more integrated into even her early writing than most people seem to expect and find. *Sensibility* was a highly contested term in her day, and she participated in debates about it. It is not at all clear that she understood reason and emotion as necessarily in conflict, as long as emotion was trained by reason and reason tempered by emotion. This question has been important to literary critics who have investigated Wollstonecraft's life, but it also has important political implications; indeed, some of her most important writing on the subject takes place in the context of debating with Burke's *Reflections* and writing her history of the French Revolution.

Wollstonecraft's writing, then, is at least as important in understanding the development of feminist theory as has often been suggested, but her work also speaks to some important debates over the development of democratic theory. But even here, her writing is distinctive, largely because of the explicit perspective of one who speaks from and about women's experiences. I will argue that her life as a woman had a clear impact on her work as a political theorist, just as the canonical theorists' lives as men had an impact on theirs. It is unfortunately common for the lives of political theorists to be ignored, as though their texts might just as well have emanated from disembodied presences. It is impossible to ignore Wollstonecraft's life, partly because her sex makes her stand apart so dramatically from other theorists.

The fact of her womanhood brings her life to our attention in a way that would not be true if she were male. But the fact that biography seems to be imposed on our vision when considering a *female* theorist could perhaps remind us to consider the significance of *male* theorists' lives even if their more normal bodies (for theorists, that is), don't remind us to think of their material existence.

Wollstonecraft was remarkable not just for her intellectual life but for the quality of what some might call her "witness politics." Her writing was in every sense a part of her life. She tried to make her mind, passions, and day-to-day choices conform to what she thought was right. She persistently noted the special difficulties of doing this as a woman, given the "state of society" on these matters, and some later interpreters use her struggles to represent the impact of society on women in her day.[14] Indeed, Wollstonecraft interpreters have devoted considerably more effort to interpreting Wollstonecraft's life than the substance of her writings. At the time of this writing there have been twenty-three full-length works devoted in major part to Wollstonecraft as a subject. The vast majority, including one play and one fiction, focus almost entirely on her life and offer little analysis of her writing beyond plot descriptions. Wollstonecraft's life has played an important role in the history of feminism as a symbol that has been used for the purposes of both feminists and antifeminists.[15]

I emphasize the complexity, nuances, and texture of Wollstonecraft's work; I will not characterize her neatly as one kind or another of political or feminist theorist. It is considerably more important and interesting to show the range of ways in which her work was related to other themes, traditions, and theorists. It is also important to recognize the ways in which she reached her own conclusions and syntheses, which are not summarized adequately by partisan labels.

Methods and Choices

The majority of my readers will have read relatively little of Wollstonecraft's writing. Among those who have read some, most will have read the *Vindication of the Rights of Woman* and only that. For this reason, and because the more I have read the less happy I have become with conventional secondary interpretations, I have incorporated more frequent and more extensive quotations from her writing into my text than is customary.

I also use relatively extensive quotations as a means to pursue another goal: allowing my subject's words to compete with my interpretation of them. The recent influence of post-structuralism seems to give permission, at least to the cruder interpreters, to play with other people's texts as they wish. In contrast, I see an ethical dimension to the relationship among writers that requires treating others' writing as we would wish our own to be treated (assuming, that is, one can accept criticism). The idea of a republic of letters, in which writers hold conversations across time and space, is too good to abandon. Wollstonecraft is not here to answer back, but if her works were commonly read and taught I could assume the corrective value of widespread primary contact with her writing by my readers. That is not the case.

No matter how careful a secondary writer is, of course, the process of ripping out bits, rearranging, and recontextualizing them, necessarily alters their character. I have been especially careful to incorporate passages that I know have been variously interpreted or that are especially subject to multiple interpretations. Some of the early chapters are perhaps more exegetical in character than I had planned when I began this project, but I found my sense of the structure and logic of her writing was quite different from most of the interpretations I had read.

Most studies of Mary Wollstonecraft approach her writing work-by-work, individually and chronologically, primarily because this interpretive literature is substantially biographical, and partly because this is the most common practice for writing about theorists in any case. I follow this convention only in Chapter 1, which describes her writing career as a part of her life story. That chapter offers a descriptive rendering of her life and work intended to provide the context for the remainder of the book and to assist with keeping dates, events, and works in order. It does not deal in depth with her works or their interpretation.

After Chapter 1 neither chronology nor, strictly speaking, individual works as wholes serve as major organizing principles of this work, with the partial exception of one chapter.[16] The central part of this book proceeds thematically, drawing on the full corpus of her public and private writings at once. Of course some themes, such as human development and reason, are threaded throughout her most of her writings while others, such as representative government, are concentrated in fewer texts, or even one. Thus at times I will dwell on the writing from single works to a greater degree, but that is not the same analytical task as explaining the meaning of a given work. I do not mean to suggest that Wollstonecraft's thinking was the same throughout her writing career, even though it lasted for only ten years. I note changes in her work where they are of interest here. But there is considerable continuity in her writing, and it has been seriously underestimated.

I begin the study of Wollstonecraft's theory and writing in Chapter 2 with her ideas on those things she considered the eternal elements and framework of the universe and human life: God, nature, reason, passion, and virtue. Chapters 3 and 4 proceed with human creation: social structure and institutions and especially the significance of "unnatural distinctions" among human beings, or inequality, dominance, and tyranny, and their corrupting influence on all parties in these social relations. These two chapters focus sequentially on different forms of institutionalized social relationships, beginning with those most conventionally discussed within historical democratic theory, such as rank and class, and ending with that which has been least central to mainstream democratic theory: gender. This movement from one form of social relationship to the next should make clear both how Wollstonecraft treated these relationships analogously within the same theoretical framework, but also how she saw them as interrelated and, to a large degree, inseparable.

In Chapter 5 an exploration of the individual, family, and state, revolving around the theme of the public and private in Wollstonecraft's writing, shows how individuals become bound into the social world and treats the problem of the distinction of "the political" from other social relationships. Both issues have been crucial in critiques of liberal theory, including liberal feminism. I continue the turn to politics, with a discussion of language politics and representation in Chapter 6 and political action and change in Chapter 7. The former chapter focuses extensively on Wollstonecraft's political debate with the master theorist of aesthetics, Edmund Burke, while the latter concludes with her reactions to the violence of the French Revolution.

The final two chapters offer my more general conclusions about Wollstonecraft's work and significance, first in the context of feminist theory (Chapter 8), then in the context of more canonical democratic political theory (Chapter 9). These chapters consider two different ways of assessing Wollstonecraft's legacy. One is to trace the path of influence through her successors. This would assess her legacy as part of a continuing chain of relationships among generations of theorists and scholars. As I shall argue, this task yields unusual problems in Wollstonecraft's case and probably, to some degree, in that of most feminist theorists. Although her name continued to be known in some circles, even her most famous book was rarely read for a long time after her death, in part because of the specific historical circumstances that surrounded immediate postmortem assessments. Historical reputations of writers and writings are not a simple matter of their "intrinsic merit."

A second way of assessing a theorist such as Wollstonecraft is to ask what we can learn from her work when we examine it in the context of other writers regardless of whether they shared any direct link, or in the context of what we know of later relevant history, or, indeed, when we assess other writers in the context of her work. Thus I will argue that considering Wollstonecraft as part of a larger reading of traditions of democratic political thought helps reveal the importance of gender in the other works as well as in her own. Knowing what we now know about the history of feminism and feminist movements in the nineteenth and twentieth centuries, we can see in Wollstonecraft's writing a writer struggling with problems of which she may have been only partly aware. In this way we can also reach more interesting conclusions than to say that Wollstonecraft did not go as far in some of her feminist conclusions as feminists might today.

My emphasis on the significance of Wollstonecraft's work both for feminist theory and democratic political theory should underscore my argument that the apparently widespread view that Wollstonecraft should be known exclusively for her advocacy of "women's rights" is inappropriate. Most of what she wrote was not on rights, or not on rights as most people understand the term. Most of her writing is not specifically about women. Much of her writing that is most directly about women is about gender; it is also profoundly about men. It will probably surprise many readers that not until Chapter 4 does a section of this book appear to take up "women" as the main topic, and that section is titled "Gender." This is not because I would disagree with anyone who says her writing on women is the most important part of her writing, and it is not because I believe that gender or women are of secondary importance in her work. Rather, this structure reflects my understanding of her work and of how gender fits into it. Unlike even a surprising amount of contemporary writing, Wollstonecraft thoroughly integrated women and gender into her broader conceptions of nature and human society. My delay in focusing directly on gender is an indication of my understanding of its centrality, not its marginality, in her work. By the time a reader reaches Chapter 4, that should be clear.

The implications of the diversity of the readers to whom I write are played out in a number of ways in this text. I have not assumed knowledge of the historical period in which Wollstonecraft lived; indeed, given the view of history taken by some schools of theory I cannot assume interest in her historical period or any other. Some historical details and observations seem commonplace to those familiar with the period, but they are not widely known by others.

Women's studies scholars will probably notice that my treatment is uneven in that I assume more knowledge on the part of readers about the "great men" than the "great women." I made some of these choices just after a colleague of mine told me about the time when, as a graduate student in the 1980s writing a paper on espionage, she referred to Harriet Tubman as the earliest African-American female who served as a government spy. Her political science professor wrote on her paper that he had never heard of Tubman and that her statement could not be true.[17]*

Trying to write this book for a diverse audience raised some other problems. Those approaching the subject from perspectives of feminist theory might be especially interested in placing Wollstonecraft in that context. A large proportion of Wollstonecraft scholars are especially interested in conclusions one might reach when interpreting her through the lens of literary criticism. Those whose background is more based in canonical political, democratic, or liberal theory might be more interested in placing Wollstonecraft among those traditions. Some of us dance in more than one minefield at once,[18] but this makes it even clearer that the languages, assumptions, questions, and standards of evaluation found in different disciplines and traditions of theory vary considerably. I have attempted to discuss the issues in a way that might make them clear to those with different backgrounds and to write in a language that is widely accessible.

But perhaps above all, I did not feel bound to follow the specific formulations of how one "does" theory in any one of these related disciplines. Each discipline has its own list of figures to whom one must pay tribute, its own function for footnotes, its own way of understanding what it means to read other people's writings. I have adopted practices I found most useful for my purpose and rejected others. In an effort to expand the number of layers on which this book works I have borrowed the technique of the biographer Richard Holmes, who holds a second conversation about his subject, Samuel Taylor Coleridge, in his footnotes.[19] Indeed, Wollstonecraft occasionally engaged in a similar practice.

Sources

Just as I was about to choose among editions of her work, I benefited from the publication of *The Works of Mary Wollstonecraft*, edited by Janet Todd and Marilyn Butler.[20] I have thanked them personally, but I also must thank them publicly for placing all of Wollstonecraft's known writing, with the exception of her letters, between the covers of seven volumes. When I read a review in the *London Review of Books* that implied that almost no one could possibly want *everything* of hers collected, including her translations and book reviews, I knew that Wollstone-craft was right to place faith in Providence (see Chapter 2). The careful scholarship and effort of Todd and Butler saved me the necessity of making regular trips up the A604 from Wivenhoe, Colchester to Cambridge. For the sake of simplicity, all Wollstonecraft references are to the Todd and Butler edition. The bibliography contains other recommended editions for those who want to read her work.

There are some things even the casual reader should know about the state of the sources, and some of the problems with using them. The editions of the books referenced here are the last editions published in Wollstonecraft's lifetime; where there were changes, as in the *Vindication of the Rights of Woman,* I use her final choices. At times the changes she made are of substantive interest, and I refer to them.

In some cases we must use some degree of faith that Mary Wollstonecraft's words are, indeed, her words. I have used the definitive collection of her letters, for example, edited by Ralph Wardle,[21] who notes that about one-third of these letters exist only as transcripts that underwent at least some editing. William Godwin did some of the work on them. Wollstonecraft's Victorian grandchild, Sir Percy Florence Shelley, and Lady Shelley did some extensive sterilizing of the record.[22] It is also important to remember that the record is not complete. We have no idea how many other letters were never saved; we do know that her letters to two men she loved, the Reverend Joshua Waterhouse and the painter Henry Fuseli, were destroyed. Neither the editing nor the losses could be imagined as random, and what they changed we cannot know. Surely the unedited Wollstonecraft was not more conservative and cautious than the one who remains.

The translations pose another question. Wollstonecraft had strong opinions about some of these books, and some "translations" are partly adaptations. What, from these works, may we consider part of "her" corpus of work? Is it appropriate to use Wollstonecraft's translations of *other* people's writing as primary sources on which to base a reading of *her* significance as a theorist? I have treated these texts differently depending on my own judgment after considering them in the context of her other work, her life, and what she said about them. Of her translations I have treated *The Elements of Morality* most like her original works. It fits very coherently, and she changed parts of the original, sometimes in subtle ways, to reflect her own point of view. I have been more selective with the others.

The reviews raise a different problem. In the *Analytical Review,* in which she did all or most of her reviewing, articles were signed only with secret codes that were not individuals' initials. There has been a lively debate over which are Wollstonecraft's reviews. I have trusted Todd and Butler's acceptance of the widely held view that Wollstonecraft showed up as M., W., and T. The most important reviews, those which I have used the most, have so much the flavor of Wollstonecraft's pen that if she didn't write them she should have.

Acknowledgments

Some of the people who were most helpful to me in the course of working on this book are, I am sure, unaware of the contributions they made. It has often been remarked (in feminist circles) that feminist writers are almost obsessive about acknowledgments, reaching back to their kindergarten teachers who let them play with trucks. In my case the story of this book begins with a directed study I took in graduate school, in which Alfred Meyer allowed me to wander off to study the development of liberal theory. There I met Mary Wollstonecraft, wrote my first paper on her, and resolved to return to her some day. It took fifteen years, but I did it.

Lisa Freeman was important in ways she understands.

A number of people have read the manuscript in part or whole, sat through brainstorming sessions with me, or provided other help for which I am grateful, including Leonore Davidoff, Nancy Kaiser and Gerda Lerner. Molly Shanley gave me a very helpful reading. I would like especially to thank my colleagues Booth Fowler, Patrick Riley, Marion Smiley, and Bernie Yack who not only read and commented on the manuscript but because of proximity had to suffer my regular babbling about it.

John Tryneski saved an author from herself. I have enjoyed working with him and the others at the University of Chicago Press involved in this book.

As usual, Graham Wilson has been a wonderful companion throughout, and even joined me in searching out Wollstonecraft's London haunts and in sitting in front of her portrait until the guards became suspicious. For his reading, conversation, and the other things too profound to mention here, I dedicate this book to him.

Madison, Wisconsin
1991

ONE

LIFE AND WORKS

*When I have more strength I read Philosophy—and write—I hope you have
not forgot that I am an Author. (Letters* 1787:155)

elating the facts of Mary Wollstonecraft's life is not a
simple task even if one has read the small library of
full-length biographies written between 1798, when
William Godwin published his infamous *Memoirs,*
and the mid-1970s, when a burst of biographical
writing occurred.[1] Gaps in knowledge of her life-
events remain, although every few years a literary detective solves another mystery. Why did she suddenly take off for apparently rambling
travels around Scandinavia with her infant daughter while her relationship with the baby's father was clearly on the wane?[2] Did
Wollstonecraft edit the *Female Reader,* ascribed on the cover to "Mr
Cresswick"?[3] Which anonymous reviews published in the *Analytical Review* were hers?[4] Exactly when did she have sexual relations with
William Godwin?[5] More questions of this sort remain for Wollstonecraft aficionados.

The more difficult problem is the interpretation of Wollstonecraft's life and writings, particularly for those of us interested in her
relationship to the history of politics and political theory. Feminist theorists and historians widely regard her as the first major theorist of
women's social and political condition, and certainly one of the most
important. There cannot be anyone in Anglophone women's studies,
and probably very few other feminist scholars, who do not know at least
a couple of facts about her.

A Vindication of the Rights of Woman is her best-known work, and
most of her other writings are now either ignored or regarded almost
exclusively as auxiliaries to the *Rights of Woman.* But most of

Wollstonecraft's writings are not "about" women. All contain at least some observations on the condition of women, but this is not the central focus of many. Indeed, in her time she was at least as well known for other works, including especially her last book, *Letters Written during a Short Residence in Sweden, Norway, and Denmark* (1796), as well as *A Vindication of the Rights of Men* (1790), her answer to Burke's *Reflections on the Revolution in France*. Her *Vindication of the Rights of Men* inspired a few stanzas of verse by William Roscoe (1753–1831), a Liverpool lawyer, writer, and patron of the arts, in the course of his *The Life, Death, and Wonderful Achievements of Edmund Burke:*[6]

> And lo! an Amazon stept out
> > One WOLLSTONECRAFT her name,
> Resolv'd to stop his mad career,
> > Whatever chance became.
>
> An oaken sapling in her hand,
> > Full on the foe she fell,
> Nor could his coat of rusty steel
> > Her vig'rous strokes repel.
>
> When strange to see, her conq'ring staff,
> > Returning leaves o'erspread,
> Of which a verdant wreath was wove
> > And bound around her head.

Roscoe, along with many other contemporaries, understood something of her wide sweep.

In contrast to Wollstonecraft's fame among feminist theorists, it is common to find political theorists who have only vaguely heard of her, if that. Many specialists in liberal theory are unfamiliar with her work.[7]* Writing on gender politics is virtually absent from the canon of "great works of political theory." Writing on gender by the "great men" receives relatively little attention, and writing by the "great women," few though there may have been in the earlier days of political theory, receives even less.[8]

Those who have written extensively about Wollstonecraft's life have necessarily relied on a fairly well defined and common set of materials. Even so, interpretations of her life and works vary widely. Most curious of all, as Janet Todd correctly observed, although the resurgence of feminism at both the turn into the twentieth century and the 1970s stimulated considerable literary interest in Wollstonecraft, "In neither period was there a serious study of Wollstonecraft's literary works. Instead, the life, which is remembered primarily because of the works, tends to overshadow those works, and the biographies, which should form bases for critical studies, are ends in themselves."[9]

The corpus of work on Wollstonecraft's writing is small compared with that on the events of her life. Few biographers show much evidence of having studied her texts carefully or, certainly, of having investigated the work of the writers and thinkers who influenced her most. Thus one writer has concluded, "with a handful of honourable exceptions, her work and its development are not seriously analysed, it is assumed that her life is more valid than her work, or even that it *was* her work."[10]

Wollstonecraft is repeatedly extracted from her historical period and from historical and contemporary communities of social thinkers. Many explain her works largely as expressions of her inner mind and most personal circumstances. Eleanor Flexner wrote that "Mary's viewpoint was shaped to an unusual degree, not by study or intercourse with her contemporaries, but by the circumstances of her own life and that of other women whom she knew. . . ."[11] Ralph Wardle, who wrote the first scholarly biography of this century and collected her letters, observed,

> Obviously Mary Wollstonecraft was an avid reader, but she was no scholar. The current of new and fresh ideas that she encountered . . . seems not to have inspired her to any very thorough investigation of the seminal works in the areas she was exploring; rather, she tested those ideas against her own experience and reading, then developed them in telling terms, often with the help of her general reading. When she cited an authority in the field she was treating, she usually did so only to reject his theories wholesale. That is to say, her lifelong desire for independence affected her thinking and writing as well as her conduct.[12]

Margaret George put it simply: "She never wrote a line that was not revealing of herself. . . ."[13] Her works are repeatedly criticized for their bad style, lack of order, questionable originality, and lack of humor; but praised, or at least recommended, for their insights into the life, mind, and passions of Mary Wollstonecraft.

Yet Wollstonecraft is remembered because of her writing, and the number of Wollstonecraft biographies is so large because she was a writer. The reviewer who wrote that "Wollstonecraft's life was not eventful enough to be interesting if she had written nothing"[14] was partly correct. This comment could be made about most famous writers, artists, musicians, or anyone else memorialized by biographers because of their works. The game of counterfactuals—especially of this magnitude—makes even less sense in biography than it does in history. Einstein would not have been Einstein without his physics, Duncan would not have been Duncan without her dancing, Verdi would not have been Verdi without his operas, and Wollstonecraft would not have been Wollstonecraft without her writing.[15]*

How shall we understand the life and its relationship to the works? This question is especially troublesome to one who is aware of the impact of gender on the interpretation of lives and writing, and who stands between the community of writers defined conventionally as political theorists, most based in political science, and feminist theorists, who range across many traditional disciplines.

Readings of Wollstonecraft's life, and even short descriptions of her, share an almost voyeuristic emphasis on her loves and emotional states. One can easily argue that there is special treatment accorded famous women. No matter who they were or what they did, what is ultimately of interest is their intimate relationships with men and babies. Women are interpreted as more subject to their personal relationships, emotions, and bodily functions than are men, and these aspects of their lives command a more central place in works about women than men.[16]*

Nevertheless, most feminist theory and research also rejects the notion that writing can be entirely extricated from the life of the author. Political theorists usually treat men's writing in political theory as though it is either free-floating or grounded in history, but not grounded in life stories. We are supposed to engage in critical rational analysis in light of universal truths, leaving aside the mundane, the personal, and the passionate. Feminist theorists may object that women's writing is overdetermined by the political, but they also reject this negation of the personal. Feminist theorists have criticized the conventional suppression of subjectivity in the social sciences and humanities, especially where gender—male or female—is a question.

John Stuart Mill is among the few canonical theorists who is often given some flesh even while we are most interested in his thought. Of course he made it relatively easy by writing his *Autobiography*. Likewise, Jean-Jacques Rousseau gave us his racier *Confessions*, a book Mary Wollstonecraft found compelling. But Mlle Lambercier and Mme de Warens do not play as predominant a role in cursory discussions of Rousseau's thought as Wollstonecraft's lovers play in discussions of her. Perhaps young Jean-Jacques' masochistic fantasies and his pre-Oedipal byplay with his lover "Maman" are too embarrassing and undignified for studies of a great political philosopher penned after the age of light. But more likely, it has simply become accepted practice to depersonalize and disembody political thought except when the person and body are female.

Part of the reason we pay different attention to the lives of female and male writers is that in male-dominated social activities such as political writing the gender of women is more remarkable than men's; the author's gender therefore draws our eye toward her personal life. As one group of scholars explained,

> Certainly, men are affected by the social construction of gender, but for men, gender has been an unmarked category. For a woman, however, the story is rarely told without reference to the dynamics of gender. Women's personal narratives are, among other things, stories of how women negotiate their "exceptional" gender status both in their daily lives and over the course of a lifetime. They assume that one can understand the live only if one takes into account gender roles and gender expectations. Whether she has accepted the norms or defied them, a woman's life can never be written taking gender for granted.[17]

The question is not whether to inform theory with biography, but how to do so.

Focusing on Wollstonecraft's life serves two purposes. One is to ground the writing in the experience of the writer, in order to make the construction of the writing more explicable. Even if one's theoretical stance identifies history as more important than biography for grounding political theory, the texts are not written by societies or cultures. They are written by people who are very partial media of those societies and cultures.

The fact that in this case the author is an eighteenth-century woman makes this point even more pressing. We are used to reading the works of men who had very different access to education, social and cultural networks, and means of financial and other material support than women, at least in the middle and upper classes. Given the "state of society," as Wollstonecraft often said, her gender can press us toward thinking more critically and productively about the relationship between experience and theorizing.

The second equally important reason for focusing on "the life" is that Wollstonecraft's personal history itself became a text of political theory and practice that has been interpreted and reinterpreted by

later writers and activists. From the time that Godwin revealed something of the private Wollstonecraft in the *Memoirs,* her life-events and
choices have been read and studied in much the same way that political-
theory texts, more conventionally defined, are read and studied.[18] It is
not a coincidence that women as diverse but important in women's history as Harriet Martineau, George Eliot, Virginia Woolf, Emma Goldman, and Ruth Benedict each found Wollstonecraft a figure with whom
they had to reckon.[19] Each woman was struck by the politics of
Wollstonecraft's life-choices and the politics of the public image of
women who live in the public eye. Just as we compare, contrast, and
synthesize different interpretations of political writings, so we must do
with a political—and politically interpreted—life, particularly when
the political life and political writings are so intertwined. Let us then
turn to the life-story before proceeding with the theory. In the spirit of
Wollstonecraft's own writings on the course of human life this story will
emphasize the education of Wollstonecraft, where *education* is used in
the broad sense of her formative life-experiences. I will trace some
themes of her life with important bearing on understanding her political significance. Many chronological narratives of Mary Wollstonecraft's biography are available elsewhere.[20]

Prehistory

Wollstonecraft was born in April 1759 in the East End of London near
what is now Liverpool Street Station, and died from childbirth com-
plications thirty-eight years later in her home near what is now Euston
Station. Between these two unfashionable addresses there were many
others. She spent much of her life in or near London, except six years
in early adolescence in rural Yorkshire, two years in late adolescence in
Wales, and almost two and a half years in France after she had become a
well-known writer. Her father wasted his moderate legacy during her
childhood and moved the family many times, so she never experienced
financial or geographic security for very long. She certainly never dwelt
with luxury except as a servant, first in fashionable places such as Bath
and Windsor, and later with a titled family in Cork.

Her childhood was unenviable. Beside being financially irrespon-
sible, Wollstonecraft's father was alcoholic and violent. He beat his wife
and, probably, his oldest daughter, Mary. Godwin reported that she remembered staying by her parents' door at night preparing to protect
her mother if need be, and threw herself between her father and
mother to shield her mother from blows. Wollstonecraft represented

her mother as passive, resigned, and favoring Mary's older brother, Edward (1757–c. 1800), who in turn seemed to show little affection or sibling loyalty to Mary, and may have eventually managed to keep from his sister her rightful inheritance.

The violence in Wollstonecraft's youth has been treated in many different ways. Virginia Woolf, who also had personal experience with the special injustices women experience, thought the violence had a crucial impact on Wollstonecraft. "If Jane Austen had lain as a child on the landing to prevent her father from thrashing her mother, her soul might have burnt with such a passion against tyranny that all her novels might have been consumed in one cry for justice."[21] This may be so, but Wollstonecraft would have been among the first to argue that violence rarely "causes" a sense of justice; rather, it is likely to create servility and corruption. Leaving aside the question of what caused Wollstonecraft to make the leap, she did. In her writings she often made the case for justice by bringing to her readers' attention compelling pictures of domestic violence, a feature of life more often mentioned by female than male writers.

Women who suffered from their husbands' abuse had virtually no options, largely because of the state-supported patriarchal rule of families by the male head of the household. By law, married women could not own property and they had no legal control over their children. Divorce was all but impossible until the Divorce Act of 1857, and only with parliamentary acts of 1878 and 1895 could abused women obtain legal separation. Parliamentary acts of 1873 and 1886 gave mothers the possibility of obtaining custody over their minor children.[22]

Wollstonecraft's relationship with her family remained strained all her life. She appears to have struggled for her mother's affection. Even when she nursed her mother during her last days, she never really received it. She would not see her father after she became an adult, but she helped to support him financially. Her relationship with her elder brother, Edward, was fraught with hostility. She worked hard to help her two other brothers and her two sisters receive training and positions, often using contacts such as the American radical Joel Barlow and the painter Henry Fuseli to help her out. A large part of her income went to her younger siblings, Eliza (1763–183?), Everina (1765–1841), James (1768–1806), and Charles (1770–1818). Although in her letters she constantly pined for independence, she continued to do what she could for them until late in her life.

Wollstonecraft received little formal education, spending only a few years in a country school. This was certainly not unusual for children of her class, especially girls. But it was rare among individuals who grew up to become political writers. Among those of her intellectual community, only Tom Paine, twenty years her senior and raised in a country town, seems to have had a comparably measly formal education.

Wollstonecraft was largely an autodidact, but throughout her life she found mentors who helped guide her reading and writing. Most of these mentorships constituted one aspect of a more complex friendship or even love relationship. Her friendships were the key to her education. These relationships were crucial to her throughout her life, and there is little doubt that her self-assessment at the age of fifteen was consistently true: "I am a little singular in my thoughts of love and friendship; I must have first place or none" (*Letters*, 1773–74:60) and "I cannot bear a slight from those I love" (*Letters*, 1773–74:62). These quotations hint at another aspect of her relationships: they were not only complex, not distinguishing between "personal" and "work" friends, but were demanding as well. The most important of these relationships gave opportunity, motivation, form, or substance to her work. I shall emphasize the role of these relationships throughout the remainder of this biographical sketch.

The first of her most important friendships was with Fanny Blood, slightly older than Wollstonecraft herself, whom she met as an adolescent. Blood's greater early attainments motivated Mary to sharpen her writing skills. But more important, Blood was an emotional centerpiece of Wollstonecraft's life. While Blood lived, Wollstonecraft dreamed of establishing a household with her; after Blood died in childbirth during her brief marriage, she remained a presence throughout Wollstonecraft's life. Her first daughter was named Fanny, and she apparently continued to wear a ring of Fanny's hair, which her second daughter eventually inherited. Fanny's brother George remained a friend and correspondent for many years, and Wollstonecraft gave financial assistance to her dead friend's parents.

Godwin was correct in characterizing his biography of Wollstonecraft as the tale of the "Author of the *Vindication of the Rights of Woman*"; it is this work that ultimately held her name in historical memory, at least among feminist writers and activists. That book was not simply her first major call for women's independence, it was part of her own lifelong struggle for personal independence, which for her included "being useful" and necessitated being able to support herself financially. Finding suitable work was extremely difficult for women in Wollstonecraft's day. She was aware that the options for female employment were diminishing; she noted in 1787 that the "few trades which are left, are now gradually falling into the hands of the men, and certainly they are not very respectable" (*Thoughts* 26). She thought most work available to women "humiliating" (*Thoughts* 25). She later expanded on these comments in the *Vindication of the Rights of Woman*. Women's work was generally so degrading and working women were regarded so suspiciously that "an attempt to earn their own subsistence, a most laudable one! sink[s] them almost to the level of those poor abandoned creatures who live by prostitution. For are not milliners and mantua-makers reckoned the next class?" (*VW* 218). Wollstonecraft, unlike many canonical theorists, certainly experienced a number of low-status jobs.

Wollstonecraft's work-life began in 1778, when as a nineteen-year-old she became a companion to a widow residing variously in the fashionable towns of Bath, Windsor, and Southampton. Many things led her to leave home; she outlined some in a 1779 account to a childhood friend. First she emphasized the brutality of her home life. "It is almost needless to tell you that my father's violent temper and extravagant turn of mind, was the principal cause of my unhappiness and that of the rest of the family," she wrote. "I will not say much of his ungovernable temper, tho' that has been the source of much misery to me;—his passions were seldom directed at me, yet I suffered more than any of them. . . ." In addition, her "father's affairs were so embarrassed by his misconduct that he was obliged to take the fortune that was settled on us children; I very readily gave up my part; I therefore have nothing to expect, and what is worse depend on a stranger" (*Letters* 1779:66).

An abusive household and the loss of any financial incentive to stay pushed her toward the door. Her mother once convinced her to stay home, but Wollstonecraft finally found an employer and left. At the same time there was another reason to seek financial independence: her love for Fanny Blood. "To live with this friend is the height of my ambition, and indeed it is the most rational wish I could make" (*Letters* 1779:67). She hoped to be able to establish a household with Fanny, which could only happen if she earned the needed finances.

Although a lady's companion had some access to the employer's social and cultural life (including in Wollstonecraft's case, glimpses of the Prince of Wales, who was to become King George IV), she was ultimately a servant, a position Wollstonecraft discussed repeatedly in later writings.[23] In her *Thoughts on the Education of Daughters*, for example, she wrote,

> Perhaps to be an humble companion to some rich old cousin, or what is still worse, to live with strangers, who are so intolera-

bly tyrannical, that none of their own relations can bear to live
with them, though they should even expect a fortune in rever-
sion. It is impossible to enumerate the many hours of anguish
such a person must spend. Above the servants, yet considered
by them as a spy, and ever reminded of her inferiority when in
conversation with the superiors. If she cannot condescend to
mean flattery, she has not a chance of being a favorite; and
should any of the visitors take notice of her, and she for a moment forget her subordinate state, she is sure to be reminded
of it. (*Thoughts* 25)

She left her position late in 1781 to care for her dying mother. After her mother's death she moved in with Fanny Blood and her family,
and worked with Fanny and her mother to support the family by en-
gaging in another form of women's work: sewing.

Another family crisis in the winter of 1783–84 launched
Wollstonecraft into a new phase of her life. This well-known incident
involved her sister Eliza, who married, possibly under duress, and suffered a nervous breakdown immediately after her child was born.
Eliza's husband, Meredith Bishop, called Mary in to help, but Mary became convinced that Eliza could not return to health while she was in
her husband's house. Wollstonecraft's letters describe Eliza's "violent fit
of phrenzy" and "raving fits that had not the least tincture of reason"
(*Letters* 1783:80). As she came to her decision to "rescue" Eliza from the
house, she wrote, "I must again repeat it you must be secret nothing can
be done till she leaves the house—For [Bishop's] friend Wood very
justly said that he was either a 'lion or a spannial'—I have been some
time deliberating on this—for I can't help pitying B. but misery must be
his portion at any rate until he alters himself—and that would be a mir-
acle" (*Letters* 1783:81). She and her friend Fanny Blood helped Eliza
escape from the house, where she left her baby. Even after her recovery
Eliza never returned.

Interpretations of this episode differ, offering not just conflicting
readings of Wollstonecraft but varying understandings of the condition
of women and the nature of the family in the late eighteenth century.
Four biographies from the early 1970s illustrate the range. Margaret
George, for example, grounded the incident in Wollstonecraft's personality, finding Wollstonecraft "self-righteous" and concluding that "The
whole thing is a powerful insight into her estrangement, her alienation,
from normal social convention."[24]

Three other biographers recognize the possibility of problems in
Eliza's marriage. Claire Tomalin doubted they were serious or chronic:

"Eliza and Meredith were more than likely casualties of their upbringings, she innocent and squeamish, he boorish and crude in his wooing. Mary's remark that 'he can't look beyond the present gratification' suggests a simple explanation for their trouble; if Eliza's sexual experience was confined to inept husbandly assaults, uncomfortable pregnancy, and excruciating childbirth, she may have taken refuge from the situation in her breakdown."[25] She concluded that, "Left to herself, there seems little doubt that Eliza would have returned to her repentant husband and innocent baby."[26]

Tomalin interpreted Wollstonecraft's role in the most negative light, writing that "already it sounded as though she was plotting to counter a male conspiracy with a female one."[27] She offered a jaundiced reading of Wollstonecraft's personality. "When Meredith showed signs of turning nasty she grew more cheerful, because it spared her feeling sympathetic towards him."[28] Eleanor Flexner, in contrast, psychoanalyzed her subject, speculating that "Mary was incapable of making any objective judgment of Meredith Bishop" because she saw her own father in him.[29] Only Emily Sunstein saw things very differently, arguing that "the villain of the piece is the social mores and the laws of the time, which made it impossible to remedy serious incompatibility decently."[30]

Wollstonecraft used the theme of a woman's flight from a brutal marriage in her final, unfinished, and most radical work, *The Wrongs of Woman; or, Maria,* described below. It is interesting also to find that a half century later on the other side of the Atlantic Susan B. Anthony experienced a strikingly similar incident, when a woman sought her help to flee from a brutal husband. The difficulty of escape and the social ostracism was reminiscent of Wollstonecraft's own life and fiction.[31]

Regardless of how Eliza's flight might be interpreted, Wollstonecraft, her sisters, and Fanny Blood now needed to find means of financial support. They debated alternative plans. Finally, they opened a girls' school in Newington Green and earned additional money by renting rooms. This began a new and crucial phase of Wollstonecraft's life.

Debut

Although Wollstonecraft maintained a lifelong interest in education, especially female education, she appears not to have been suited to the role of schoolmistress. She found the position of teachers unenviable: "A teacher at a school is only a kind of upper servant, who has more work than the menial ones" (*Thoughts* 25). When she later wrote that "a person of genius is the most improper person to be employed in education, public or private," one wonders whether she was thinking of herself (*VW* 137).

What was more important to Wollstonecraft's development, with her move to Newington Green in 1783, was that she had stumbled onto the base of one of the important Dissenting academies, and therefore onto the community formed around the Dissenters' religious and political affiliations. For the remainder of her life most of her friendships and intellectual relationships revolved around the loose network of people within a modest-sized but sprawling community of the mostly Dissenting political left. One can argue that her intellectual and political education truly began in this period.

Dissenters played a distinct and important role in English life at the time.[32]* Names such as Priestley, Wedgewood, Wilkinson, Cadbury, and (Erasmus) Darwin demonstrate their centrality in the growth of science and industry. As Isaac Kramnick has observed, many of the best schools in England were Dissenting academies, in part because, "Like most marginal minorities, they were preoccupied with educating the young. Only in this way could special traits be passed on from generation to generation."[33] These "special traits" are precisely the ones we tend to associate most with the bourgeois and the industrial revolution, of which the Dissenters were so much a part: usefulness, thrift, simplicity, orderliness, and a keen sense of the value of time and delayed gratification.

The Dissenters' choices of arenas for achievement and their sense of community and political views were no doubt sharpened by the limitation of civil rights and liberties imposed by law, including the seventeenth-century Test and Corporation Acts. Dissenters were barred from holding public office and from the great universities at Oxford and Cambridge. The unsuccessful battle to repeal the Test and Corporation Acts in the 1780s and 1790s served as a focal point for a larger development of liberal and radical politics. Indeed, Marilyn Butler refers to the Dissenters as the "most coherent group among the reformers" during the 1780s.[34] Wollstonecraft remained attached to the Church of England as long as she identified herself with any religion, but she was so influenced by this community and, indeed, so much a part of its social and political circle, that she is sometimes erroneously identified as a Dissenter.[35]

At Newington Green, Wollstonecraft established particularly close links with the widow of James Burgh (1714–75), whose work may have influenced her own.[36] She also became a friend and admirer of the chaplain of the group, Richard Price (1723–91), whose blessing on the French Revolution in his *Discourse on the Love of our Country* (1789) irked

Edmund Burke into writing his *Reflections on the Revolution in France* (1790). Burke's "unmanly sarcasms" (*VM*:19) directed personally against her mentor were in part responsible for the tone of writing with which Wollstonecraft answered his *Reflections* with her *Vindication of the Rights of Men.*[37]*

In 1784 Fanny Blood left for Lisbon to join her new husband, and late in 1785 Wollstonecraft was called away from her school by another crisis; she arrived in Lisbon in time to attend Fanny's death following childbirth. Childbirth was still very dangerous in eighteenth-century Europe, and most women would know it. No doubt the death of her beloved friend kept this fact in front of Wollstonecraft when she pondered questions having to do with reproduction, sexuality, and motherhood.

Wollstonecraft returned to find the school in Newington Green nearly defunct and most of the boarders gone. She carried on with a few students and penned the first manuscript that earned her money: *Thoughts on the Education of Daughters: With Reflections on Female Conduct, in the More Important Duties of Life.* With the assistance of a Newington Green friend, Wollstonecraft sold her manuscript to the London publisher Joseph Johnson for 10 guineas.

Thoughts is Wollstonecraft's first contribution to a growing genre: advice books on female education. Among her well-known predecessors were *A Father's Legacy to his Daughters* (1774), by John Gregory (1724–73), and *Sermons to Young Women* (1765), by James Fordyce (1720–96).[38] Her book, like most others of the same kind, understands the term "education" in its broad sense, including all aspects of child raising from the earliest feedings until the young woman leaves home. The book is structured as twenty-one brief chapters. Each covers a specific theme, many of which are repeated in later works: the importance of breast-feeding, the difference between external manners and true virtue, the benefits of the school of adversity, and the necessity of the education of women and the need for them to be able to support themselves, especially because they might find themselves as adults with no one to rely on but themselves.

Thoughts has received little attention and is generally regarded as valuable primarily as an early test of some of the ideas Wollstonecraft developed later and some she clearly discarded as her views become more radical. It was reprinted with an essay by Fénelon in Dublin in 1788, then was not reprinted until recently in scholarly editions.

Wollstonecraft searched for more work to support herself, and once again found one of the very few jobs open to women. In 1786, the twenty-seven-year-old arrived in Dublin to serve as a governess in an aristocratic family. Her description in *Thoughts* suggests how unhappy she was with her employment:

> A governess to young ladies is equally disagreeable. It is ten to one if they meet with a reasonable mother; and if she is not so, she will be continually finding fault to prove she is not ignorant, and be displeased if her pupils do not improve, but angry if the proper methods are taken to make them do so. The children treat them with disrespect, and often with insolence. In the mean time life glides away. . . . (*Thoughts* 25)

The nasty portraits of aristocrats she drew in her later comments on unnatural social distinctions are consistent with the bourgeois radical's view, but sometimes they are also life drawings of her former employers.[39] Despite her attitude toward this job and her employers she became particularly close to one daughter, Margaret, who years later settled in Italy with her lover under the name of Mrs. Mason, the name of the main character in Mary Wollstonecraft's *Original Stories*.

Wollstonecraft used her time as governess to read and write. She reported to her sister late in 1786, "I have so many new ideas of late, I can scarcely arrange them—I am lost in a *sea* of thoughts" (*Letters* 1786:119). The product of her writing was her first novel and second publication, *Mary, a Fiction*. In March 1787 she wrote to her sister that she was reading and enjoying Rousseau's *Émile*. "He chuses a *common* capacity to educate—and gives as a reason, that a genius will educate itself" (*Letters* 1787:145). In September she wrote to a friend, "'Spite of my vexations, I have lately written, a fiction which I intend to give to the world; it is a tale, to illustrate an opinion of mine, that a genius will educate itself" (*Letters* 1787:162). She completed it by November. When it appeared, the cover displayed a quotation from Rousseau: "L'exercice des plus sublimes vertus éleve et nourrit le génie."[40]

Wollstonecraft called *Mary* a fiction, which it surely is, but she also observed that "I have drawn from Nature" (*Letters* 1787:162). It follows the history of a young woman, Mary, who received little emotional or intellectual sustenance from her parents, and therefore had to educate herself. She develops an ardent friendship with a young woman named Ann, obviously modeled on Fanny Blood. Mary, who can think of nothing but Ann, agrees to marry a man she does not love in order to fulfill the dying wish of her mother. After their marriage, the husband leaves to finish his education, and Mary remains with Ann, who is becoming classically tubercular. The pair leaves for Lisbon to help Ann's health, and along the way Mary meets her true love, Henry. Ann dies, and Mary and Henry return to England and carry on their very platonic love, although "had Ann lived, it is probable she would never have loved Henry so fondly; but if she had, she could not have talked of her passion to any human creature" (55). Henry, whose constitution is weak, also dies and Mary is faced with the prospect of living with her husband. She agrees to live with him if she is given one year to travel on her own. The novel closes with her joy at the knowledge that she will soon die from the burdens of life, and that "she was hastening to that world *where there is neither marrying,* nor giving in marriage" (73; emphasis in the original).

Mary began *Mary* a little more than a year after the death of Fanny, and the passages about Ann are poignant tributes to her friend. Where *Thoughts* was written specifically to earn money, *Mary* was a labor of love and the first time we see the play of intellect and passion in her work. Godwin claimed that all events in the novel that do not relate to Fanny are fictional, but the entire work is a jumble of names and characters that are recognizable from her life, not the least of which is the aptly named protagonist.

It is difficult to give any sense of plot without causing amusement; moreover most commentators note how badly written it is. It was not reprinted until the 1970s. At the same time it is a mistake to dismiss the book. It contains many of her customary themes developed later. Here she first defined and argued against female propriety, and stated her preference for work over the slavery of marriage. Most commentators have agreed that "*Mary* makes manifest Mary Wollstonecraft's situation; that of a passionate, neurotic woman whose puritanism and sense of moral and intellectual superiority block her emotional and physical demands."[41] Unfortunately, few have noticed along with Miriam Brody Kramnick that in this work "Wollstonecraft is no ideologue yet, but reading *Mary* one meets the incipient female revolutionary."[42]

When Wollstonecraft was fired from her position as governess, she returned to London and, with the aid of the publisher Joseph Johnson, turned herself over to writing as a means of support. Johnson (1738–1809) played a crucial role in Wollstonecraft's development. He was a radical Dissenting publisher, whose shop, publications list, and home served as the meeting place for a significant portion of the London left (plus foreign "visitors" such as Benjamin Franklin and Condorcet) through the mid-1780s and French Revolution. Beside Wollstonecraft, his circle included Joseph Priestley (1733–1804), William Blake, Thomas Paine, Thomas Christie (1761–96), William Godwin, Henry Fuseli (1741–1825), Anna Laetitia Barbauld (1743–1825), and John Horne Tooke (1736–1812). "There were not many oppressed groups among his contemporaries who did not find a champion under his imprint: slaves, Jews, Dissenters, women, victims of the game laws and press gangs, little chimney sweeps, college fellows barred from matrimony, animals ill-used, the disenfranchised and the simply poor and hungry."[43]

Johnson made her a regular part of this circle, advanced her loans when she needed them, and even gave her a place to live when she returned to London. She wrote to her sister in 1787 that Johnson, "whose uncommon kindness, I believe, has saved me from despair . . . assured me that if I exert my talents in writing I may support myself in a comfortable way" (*Letters*, 1787:164).

In late 1787 Wollstonecraft reported that she was finishing another book, published in 1788 as *Original Stories from Real Life: With Conversations Calculated to Regulate the Affections and Form the Mind to Truth and Goodness*. This book was aimed at young people as part of their moral education. As Wollstonecraft wrote, "These conversations and tales are accommodated to the present state of society; which obliges the author to attempt to cure those faults by reason, which ought never to have taken root in the infant mind" (*Stories* 359).[44*] Wollstonecraft believed most parents were not taking the care they should to impart to children proper habits of virtue and reason. The story follows the good teacher Mrs. Mason as she attempts to teach the young motherless sisters Mary and Caroline their lessons. Each chapter contains a different lesson imparted to the two girls and, presumably, their readers. The second edition included six striking plates designed and engraved by William Blake.[45]

Wollstonecraft's children's book must be understood in the context of the genre and the ideological purposes it served during the late eighteenth century.[46] The notion of a distinct children's literature developed at that time, especially within Dissenting circles. Books aimed specifically at children were increasingly seen as valuable vehicles for training children in appropriate values and behavior. Her book, including its rather dour character, is not unique for its type, although one critic of this school of children's literature thinks *Original Stories* "has a strong claim to be the most sinister, ugly, overbearing book for children ever published."[47*]

According to William Godwin, 1787 was also the year that Wollstonecraft began her unfinished fiction, *Cave of Fancy*, which is said to draw on Samuel Johnson's *Rasselas*.[48*] In this fragment an old sage living in a rude hut on a faraway mountain finds and adopts an orphan whom he names "Sagesta" after himself. The fragment suggests the book was to be about her education.

By the end of the year Wollstonecraft was clearly defining herself professionally. She had begun this process earlier; while she was working on *Mary* she had already defined herself as an Author (*Letters* 1787:155). She announced her intentions in a letter to her sister Everina. After a discussion of her financial problems she turned to her plans: "Before I go on will you pause—and if after deliberating you will promise not to mention to *any one* what you know of my designs (*though you may think my requesting you to conceal them unreasonable*) I will trust to your honor—and proceed." Wollstonecraft then tells her that Johnson had suggested she might support herself by writing. "I am then going to be the first of a new genus—I tremble at the attempt yet if I fail—I *only* suffer" (*Letters* 1787:164).

After once again requesting silence on the matter, she wrote, "My undertaking would subject me to ridicule—and an *inundation* of *friendly* advice, to which I cannot listen—I must be independant." And finally, "And freedom *even* uncertain freedom—is dear. I shall watch for the post—I should have written before but I wait[ed] till I was determined what course to pursue, if I had any good to communicate, I should not have been so tardy. This project has *long* floated in my mind. You know I am not born to trod in the beaten track—the peculiar bent of my nature pushes me on" (*Letters* 1787:165).

Wollstonecraft defined herself as the "first of a new genus," a woman supporting herself by writing, although she was still nervous about public reaction to this definition. Godwin noted in the *Memoirs* that, "At the commencement of her literary career, she is said to have conceived a vehement aversion to the being regarded, by her ordinary acquaintance, in the character of an author, and to have employed some precautions to prevent its occurrence."[49] The point is not that women did not write. We now know there were many English women writers by the time Wollstonecraft picked her path.[50] Wollstonecraft clearly did not know how many, but her book reviews reveal no surprise at the number of women's works she read. Rather, her anxiety likely stemmed from her choice of writing as a profession, as a means of supporting and publicly defining herself. It was not yet common for women to put their names on the title pages of their books, and writing was presumably an inappropriate way for a "lady" to support herself, although of course there were precious few of these ways. Wollstonecraft had tried and rejected most that were available.

In 1788 Wollstonecraft's work schedule became hectic. She translated Jacques Necker's *De L'Importance des Opinions Religieuses* from the French. She thought it a "work of importance" as she worked on it (*Let-*

ters 1788:174), and her anonymous review of her own translation was favorable, "though the author does not appear uniformly ingenious and perspicuous" (*Revs* 1789:66). By the time she wrote her history of the French Revolution, her assessment of the former controller general of finance's character had harshened:

> Having written on a subject, that naturally attracted the attention of the public, he had the vanity to believe, that he deserved the exaggerated applause he received, and the reputation of wise, when he was only shrewd. Not content with the fame he acquired by writing on a subject . . . he wished to obtain a higher degree of celebrity, by forming into a large book various metaphysical shreds of arguments, which he had collected from the conversation of men, fond of ingenious subtilties; and the style, excepting some declamatory passages, was as inflated and confused as the thoughts were far fetched and unconnected. (*FrRev* 42)

Joseph Johnson's biographer observed that this work "served both to enhance the French minister's reputation and, coincidentally, to reassure English readers that spirituality and finance were not incompatible."[51] Wollstonecraft's translation would have served as the vehicle. Despite her opinion of Necker himself (1732–1804), the work she translated appears to be substantially consistent with her own religious views.

During the same year Joseph Johnson and Thomas Christie (1761–96), a Scottish Unitarian, founded the *Analytical Review*, a monthly devoted primarily to reviews of books, pamphlets, plays, and poetry. The journal took its political flavor from the Johnson circle, and Wollstonecraft became a reviewer and, eventually, editorial assistant for it. The sheer number of reviews she contributed between 1788 and 1797 is impressive; they also provide a usually neglected resource for understanding the thinking of Mary Wollstonecraft. These reviews plus translations offered her the hope of financial independence.

Unfortunately, because reviews in the *Analytical Review* were anonymous, identifying Wollstonecraft's contributions takes educated guesswork and is the subject of some controversy.[52] Reviewers used initials as signatures that, in some cases, must have had a very private meaning indeed. Scholarly consensus identifies Wollstonecraft's usual notations as M., W., and T. Gerald Tyson cautioned us against reading too much political meaning into the anonymity, arguing that this practice "became established not as a protection against an action for libel but because contributions to periodicals were considered beneath the dignity of most writers: to acknowledge authorship to this sort was tantamount to admitting that one lived in Grub Street."[53]

Wollstonecraft's writing during this period suggests she was working in Grub Street style, accepting any writing to support herself. Her reviewing was important in other ways: It probably served as partial replacement for the formal education she never really had. Her subjects included but were not limited to novels, plays, works on education and travel, and even some natural history. The fictions she reviewed included the influential works of Robert Bage, Fanny Burney (as well as one by Burney's sister Sarah and the important music history of her father, Charles Burney), Thomas Day, Elizabeth Inchbald, Charlotte Lennox, Jacques Henri Bernardin de Saint-Pierre, Charlotte Smith, Helen Maria Williams, the plays of her friend Thomas Holcroft, essays and pedagogical works by Mme Genlis, Samuel Johnson, Catharine Macaulay, Sarah Trimmer, and other works by authors as diverse as the Comtesse du Barry, Olaudah Equiano, William Gilpin, Hester Lynch Piozzi, Richard Price, Jean-Jacques Rousseau, and William Smellie.

Some of her reviews are long and display considerable critical thought, as in her reviews of Rousseau's *Confessions;* others follow the common practice of the day, offering little more than plot summaries and quotations, and some were brief and pointed, as was her review of *To the Feeling Heart. Exalted Affection; or Sophia Pringle,* by the Rev. W. Cole, printed here in full: "A laboured attempt to be pathetic is here introduced with due ceremony to the reader; but we are at a loss to know, whether the title alludes to Sophia's exalted affection for heaven, or her lover" (*Revs* 1790:202). Her anonymity did not hide the wit that some of her friends noted and some later interpreters missed. Wollstonecraft wrote about 290 reviews between June 1788, the first issue to which she contributed, and the end of 1790, when she published *A Vindication of the Rights of Men.*

In 1789 Wollstonecraft published another full-length work aimed at children: *A Female Reader: Or, Miscellaneous Pieces in Prose and Verse; Selected from the Best Writers and Disposed under Proper Heads; for the Improvement of Young Women* (1789). The title page lists the author as "Mr. Cresswick, Teacher of Elocution," although the evidence found in Joseph Johnson's papers and Godwin's *Memoirs* has lead most people to accept Wollstonecraft as the author.[54]

As the preface says, the volume was modeled after *The Speaker* (1774) by William Enfield, a tutor at the Warrington Dissenting Academy. The two works shared the view that rhetorical exercise is an important part of education.

> The main object of this work is to imprint some useful lessons on the mind, and cultivate the taste at the same time—to infuse a relish for a pure and simple style, by presenting natural and touching descriptions from the Scriptures, Shakspeare, etc. Simplicity and sincerity generally go hand in hand, as both proceed from a love of truth. (*Reader* 55)

Wollstonecraft praised Enfield for initiating a methodical order on the individual pieces in his collection; she defined her contribution as readapting the model to the purpose of female education. She divided the work into six books containing Narrative Pieces; Didactic and Moral Pieces; Allegories and Pathetic Pieces; Dialogues, Conversations, and Fables; Descriptive Pieces; and Devotional Pieces and Reflections on Religious Objects. Other than the Bible and Shakespeare, we find contributions from, among others, William Cowper, Hester Chapone, Mme Genlis, John Gregory, her acquaintances Anna Laetitia Barbauld and Sarah Trimmer, Johann Kaspar Lavater, and herself. Her own contributions included the preface, three selections from *Thoughts on the Education of Daughters,* and four original prayers.

Taken as a whole, the content of the *Reader* comfortably represents the social and pedagogical views of Dissenting social thinkers and educators, with Wollstonecraft's own emphasis on women's education. The views on women are not completely conventional but certainly are more so than they would be within the ensuing few years. Wollstonecraft's developing radical politics begin to emerge more clearly in this volume. In a work that emphasizes order and connection among ideas, it is instructive to see a poem entitled "On Slavery," by William Cowper ("And what man seeing this,/ And having human feelings, does not blush/ And hang his head, ...") followed by the same author's "The Bastile" ("The shame to manhood, and opprobrious more/ To France than all her losses and defeats,/ . . . Her house of bondage, worse than that of old/ Which God aveng'd on Pharoah—the Bastile") (*Reader* 297–301). Wollstonecraft's *Reader* was ostensibly aimed at creating good habits of mind but also some training in what she would view as good habits of politics.

In 1790 Wollstonecraft worked on three more translations. One, an abridged translation of *Physiognomy,* by Johann Kaspar Lavater (1741–1801), never appeared in print. Although the work was lost, her effort ties together a series of related anecdotes that illustrates some of the flavor of researching Wollstonecraft's life.[55]* Lavater and the painter Henry Fuseli had been best friends in Zurich, and both had left after their involvement in a political row. Fuseli later sent graphic love letters to Lavater recalling their earlier times together, even tempting Lavater when he was newly wed. Fuseli also translated Lavater's *Aphorisms*, selections of which appeared in Wollstonecraft's *Female Reader*.

Their mutual friend Thomas Holcroft managed to produce and publish his translation of *Physiognomy* before Wollstonecraft; Fuseli started a literary row by panning it in the pages of the *Analytical Review*. Within a year a Samuel Shaw had the temerity to publish an abridgment of Holcroft's translation; Wollstonecraft reviewed it in the *Analytical Review* in 1792, the same year she met Lavater in London.[56] She began her review by observing, "This is one of those surreptitious publications, by means of which authors . . . are deprived of their legal right, [in order] to gratify the rapacity of needy book-makers, or the impatience of frugal readers." She ended with, "it is one of those contemptible catchpennies that cannot be too severely reprehended" (*Revs* 450). At the same time Wollstonecraft was in the midst of falling in love with Fuseli.

The principles of physiognomy, including the ability to read individuals' characters on their faces, played additional roles in Wollstonecraft's life. A major section of *The Cave of Fancy* is devoted to the sage reading the bodies of the victims of a shipwreck. She used these principles elsewhere as well (e.g. *Reader* 59). Within a few weeks of her death, Godwin received an analysis of the character of their infant that used Lavater's principles of physiognomy. The fitting epigraph to this series of observations was written by Johann Carl Schweitzer, a pro-revolution Swiss banker and friend of Wollstonecraft in Paris, whose wife, not incidentally, had been the object of Fuseli's amorous attentions. After Wollstonecraft died Schweitzer wrote to Fuseli: "Ich meld es zum Elysium/ Wollstonecraft und Lavatern, es sei/ Das hart'ste Erz zu deinem Bild—dein Herz!" [I announce to Wollstonecraft and Lavater in Elysium that in any portrait of you the hardest element must be your heart].[57]*

The next of Wollstonecraft's translations appeared in only one edition and has appeared equally unremarkable to later scholars. *Young Grandison. A Series of Letters from Young Persons to Their Friends* is a translation of the Dutch work by Maria Geertuida de Werken de Cambon. It is an epistolary novel, one of the many literary descendants of Samuel Richardson's *History of Sir Charles Grandison* (1753–54). The main character is William D———, a friend of young Charles Grandison's.

The far more successful and important work was Wollstonecraft's 1790 translation of Christian Gotthilf Salzmann's *Moralisches elementar-*

buch (1782) as *Elements of Morality, for the Use of Children; with an introductory address to parents,* illustrated by William Blake. Wollstonecraft explained her translation: "This little Work fell accidentally into my hands, when I began to learn German, and, merely as an exercise in that language, I attempted to translate it; but, as I proceeded, I was pleased to find that chance had thrown in my way a very rational book, and that the writer coincided with me in opinion respecting the method which ought to be pursued to form the heart and temper, or, in other words, to inculcate the first principles of morality." Further, she wrote, "I term it a translation, though I do not pretend to assert that it is a literal one. . . ." She claimed to have made a number of changes, including resetting it in England and giving it a more English—and presumably less German—flavor. "My reason for naturalizing it must be obvious—I did not wish to puzzle children by pointing out modifications of manners, when the grand principles of morality were to be fixed on a broad basis" (*Elements* 5).

After a brief introduction to parents, the book follows Mr. and Mrs. Jones and their two children, Charles and Mary, through their adventures. Each chapter's adventure has a moral point to impart. Wollstonecraft assisted the didactic intention of the book by presenting a sketch of the lessons at the end in index form. The first part concerns Duties to Ourselves, divided according to the Body and the Soul. This is followed by Duties to Others, including God and Men. The third part concerns Duties to Animals, and the last two parts focus on Things (primarily food and dress) and Events (agreeable and disagreeable). The list of elements of morality Wollstonecraft included offers a sketch of the new bourgeois ideology, but its especially liberal version. One of the clearest lessons, for example, is the virtue of religious toleration. The type of religious parochialism chosen as the example in the book is anti-Semitism (*Elements* 148–50, 183–84). Salzmann approved of the translation; in return he translated the *Vindication of the Rights of Woman* into German.[58]*

While most of her later readers have found these works remarkable primarily for their substantive mediocrity or stylistic faults, this period of extraordinary literary activity is important for today's observers to understand. William Godwin, who well understood the experience of hack writing, was probably speaking very personally when he observed about this period of her life,

> It perhaps deserves to be remarked that this sort of miscellaneous literary employment, seems . . . rather to damp and contract, than to enlarge and invigorate, the genius. The

writer is accustomed to see his performances answer the mere mercantile purpose of the day, and confounded with those of persons to whom he is secretly conscious of a superiority. No neighbour mind serves as a mirror to reflect the generous confidence he felt within himself; and perhaps the man never yet existed, who could maintain his enthusiasm to its full vigour, in the midst of this kind of solitariness. He is touched with the torpedo of mediocrity. I believe that nothing which Mary produced during this period, is marked with those daring flights, which exhibit themselves in the little fiction she composed just before its commencement.[59]

Godwin reminded his readers that Wollstonecraft was not just financially responsible for herself but for much of her family as well. It is unfortunately rare to take account of theorists' material conditions in evaluating their corpus of work, as Godwin demanded we do. More often, it seems we are to assume that writers were allowed by circumstance to write only their best. Indeed, Wollstonecraft herself took day-to-day circumstances into account in her assessment of Rousseau. She appeared impressed with his struggles "To secure his independance, and to endeavour to earn his daily bread, without prostituting his talents . . ." (*Revs* 1790:231).

At the same time, Godwin believed this period of intense writing made important contributions to Wollstonecraft's development as a writer and thinker. He thought "the uninterrupted habit of composition gave a freedom and firmness to the expression of her sentiments," and that the company she kept during that period "nourished her understanding, and enlarged her mind." Finally, he believed that the French Revolution "did not fail to produce a conspicuous effect in the progress of Mary's reflections."[60] Others have agreed. One Wollstonecraft biographer, for example, argued that during this time in the late 1780s Wollstonecraft "went from gifted, anxious, naive amateur to disciplined, self-assured, versatile professional in a competitive field, an accomplishment unmatched by any woman at that time."[61]

Vindications

Wollstonecraft's next work, arguably her first great one, was published at the end of 1790. On 1 November Edmund Burke published his *Reflections on the Revolution in France,* which had existed in manuscript at least since February. Within a week the first of approximately seventy responses appeared. On 29 November an anonymous *Vindication of the*

Rights of Men appeared; the second edition was published under the name Mary Wollstonecraft. Although we can see the roots of this production in earlier writings, Mary Poovey correctly identifies one aspect of this first vindication that cannot be ignored: "Significantly, her first extensive production as a self-supporting professional and self-proclaimed intellectual took the form that most people would have considered the least appropriate for a woman—the political disquisition. Requiring knowledge of government (in which women had no share), analytical ability (of which women theoretically had little) and the ambition to participate directly in contemporary events (of which women were supposed to have none), political disquisition was in every sense a masculine domain."[62]

The reaction of the reviewer in the *Critical Review* in December testifies to the historical political significance of Wollstonecraft's effort:

> It has been observed in an old play, that minds have no sex; and in truth we did not discover this Defender of the Rights of *Man* to be a *Woman*. The second edition, however, which often reveals secrets, has attributed this pamphlet to Mrs. Wollstonecraft, and if she assumes the disguise of a man, she must not be surprised that she is not treated with the civility and respect that she would have received in her own person. As the article was written before we saw the second edition, we have presented an acknowledgment of this kind to the necessary alterations. It would not have been sufficient to have corrected merely verbal errors: a Lady should have been addressed with more respect.[63]

It is notable that publishing a political tract anonymously, that is, without an identity, was to this critic the same as assuming "the disguise of a man." The disguise, presumably, is not the gap on the title page, but the political tract as a genre which, as Poovey argues, was viewed as essentially masculine and, indeed, probably still is when it does not address "women's" questions as the main theme.[64]*

Wollstonecraft explains the occasion of her writing, "Mr. Burke's Reflections on the French Revolution first engaged my attention as the transient topic of the day; and reading it more for amusement than information, my indignation was roused by the sophistical arguments, that every moment crossed me, in the questionable shape of natural feelings and common sense. Many pages of the following letter were the effusions of the moment" (*VM* 5).

Later writers are nearly universal in their condemnation of this first vindication as a rushed, unscholarly, personal, emotional diatribe against a great political thinker, or at least as a most uneven match for the talents of Burke. At the same time, many have found something compelling about it. As Emily Sunstein writes, "If her book was intemperate, emotional, and exaggerated, it was precisely the kind of topical, personalized, fiery polemic on which political controversy thrives. It was snatched up by friend and foe, made an extraordinary impact, and sold out at once."[65] It may be no coincidence that in her lecture on Wollstonecraft as a feminist model, Emma Goldman picked out passages of this piece as particularly important.[66]

Wollstonecraft's critics are correct in one respect: the *Vindication of the Rights of Men* is an attack on Edmund Burke more than it is a defense of the French Revolution, which she saved for later. But even in this respect her work has been widely misunderstood and, as I shall argue more thoroughly below, seriously underestimated.[67] She certainly paid Burke in kind and with interest for his personal attacks on Richard Price. She argued against the Burke who was a prime advocate of a political argument which she found not simply disagreeable but immoral and impious. She seized the language politics of Burke's writings, and debated him on this ground. In the end—rather, in the first paragraph—she argued with Burke's earlier *Enquiry into the Origin of Our Ideas of the Sublime and the Beautiful* (1757) almost as much as she argued with the *Reflections*. Her *Rights of Men* was not merely a rude polemic but one of the most sophisticated essays on political argument and political psychology of her day and some time after. This aspect of her pamphlet has been overlooked by almost all commentators.[68]

The *Vindication of the Rights of Men* was followed by Mary Wollstonecraft's most famous work, the *Vindication of the Rights of Woman, with Strictures on Moral and Political Subjects* (1792). This work was also written quickly but not in response to any particular stimulus. It is much more the culmination of her earlier work, combining the concern with women's condition and education found in her earliest works and the more general political theory found in the *Vindication of the Rights of Men*. As she wrote it, she seemed to know this book would be special. In October 1791 she wrote to her friend William Roscoe with regard to a portrait of her he had commissioned:

> Be it known unto you, my dear Sir, that I am actually sitting for the picture and that it will be shortly *forthcoming*. I do not imagine that it will be a very striking likeness; but, if you do not find

me in it, I will send you a more faithful sketch—a book that I am now writing, in which *I* myself, for I cannot *yet* attain to Homer's dignity, shall certainly appear, head and heart—but this is between ourselves—pray respect a woman's secret. (*Letters* 202–3)

The portrait in paint pictures a handsome, self-assured woman with powdered hair and small ruffs at the wrist; the portrait in print pictures the same woman, but without the powder and ruffs.[69]*

Wollstonecraft submitted the final pages of the *Rights of Woman* 2 January 1792, and the same day wrote another letter to Roscoe.

I shall give the last sheet to the printer to day; and, I am dissatisfied with myself for not having done justice to the subject.— Do not suspect me of false modesty—I mean to say, that had I allowed myself more time I could have written a better book, in every sense of the word, the length of the Errata vexes me—as you are a gentleman author you can make some allowance for a little ill humour at seeing such a blur, which would only make those, who have never dabbled in ink, smile. I intend to finish the next volume before I begin to print, for it is not pleasant to have the Devil coming for the conclusion of a sheet before it is written. Well, I have said enough of this said book—more than is civil, and not sufficient to carry off the fumes of ill humour which makes me quarrel with myself. (*Letters* 205–6)

The *Rights of Woman* had gone to the printer bit by bit as she wrote, which either means she must have written as convention claims Mozart did—first in the head, then in final form on paper—or the list of errata must indeed have made an author's heart sink. Despite the apologies, her letter reveals confidence in her skill and chosen profession, but also recognition of the difference between the "gentleman" author, such as Roscoe, who could write as an amateur in the literal sense of the word, and a professional author such as herself, whose pen was her livelihood.

Thoughts on the Education of Daughters was a treatise on women's education by a daughter of the Enlightenment; the *Vindication of the Rights of Woman* was written by a sister of the French Revolution, although one who did not know that the Revolution would do precious little for women as such. It is dedicated to Charles Maurice de Talleyrand-Périgord (1754–1838), one time bishop and active politician of the French Revolution, who published a proposal for education in the new

France that dissatisfied Wollstonecraft with respect to its plan for women. The *Rights of Woman,* therefore, is covered with a letter to Talleyrand asking that her treatise be considered as an argument for revision of the French constitution. The treatise itself, however, is addressed in large part to women, especially middle-class women.[70] In this work Wollstonecraft not only did not disguise her sex, but made a point of identifying herself as a woman within the text, as when she referred to "my sex" in discussing its condition or her aspirations for it.[71]

Wollstonecraft specifically linked her work to previous books on female education and manners, but criticized the others because of her belief that "the books of instruction, written by men of genius, have had the same tendency as more frivolous productions" (*VW* 73). Much of the body of the book is a critical review of the best-known works.

Wollstonecraft begins with a catechism of the Enlightenment:

> In what does man's pre-eminence over the brute creation consist? The answer is as clear as that a half is less than the whole; in Reason.
>
> What acquirement exalts one being over another? Virtue; we spontaneously reply.
>
> For what purpose were the passions implanted? That man by struggling with them might attain a degree of knowledge denied to the brutes; whispers Experience.
>
> Consequently the perfection of our nature and capability of happiness, must be estimated by the degree of reason, virtue, and knowledge, that distinguish the individual, and direct the laws which bind society: and that from the exercise of reason, knowledge and virtue naturally flow is equally undeniable, if mankind be viewed collectively. (*VW* 81)

She followed this discussion of the human condition and character with one on "sexual" condition and character and other corruptions of human character based on "unnatural distinctions."[72]

The treatise's main theme throughout is the role of education in the development of human character and virtue. The emphasis on education has often been misunderstood. Although an important chapter of the book—indeed, perhaps the most famous—is "On National Education," the use of the term, "education" is not the current restricted notion of instruction, particularly in schools, but the broader sense more common in her day, more like our current conceptions of "child-raising" or "socialization." The unfortunate result of this common misinterpretation is that Wollstonecraft is often posed as offering "only" education (meaning formal schooling) as the solution to women's problems. In this sense her work would not be highly unusual for its day. In fact she acknowledged her debt to Catharine Macaulay, whose *Letters on Education* (1790) she had reviewed (*Revs* 1790:309–22), as well as Thomas Day's *The History of Sandford and Merton* (1789), which she had also reviewed (*Revs* 1789:174–76). The *Rights of Woman* is not beautifully written, but it appears extraordinarily disorganized only if one interprets it mainly as an argument about education narrowly conceived. The text certainly does not drive us to consideration of schools in any linear fashion, and there is a whole further chapter on another subject after she dispenses with her school plan.[73]

I will argue that Wollstonecraft's most widely read work is in some ways her least understood. One reading of the book is that it called for extending the "rights of man" to women, leading to an interpretation of Wollstonecraft as the consummate liberal of the later Enlightenment. In fact she called for extending the political analysis of the Dissenting radicals and their associates among the French beyond governmental institutions and public politics to the family and private politics. She was a consummate anti-patriarchal thinker in a way few better-known "anti-patriarchal" thinkers have been or could even understand.[74]

Regina Janes has traced the history of the reception of the *Rights of Woman,* demonstrating that contrary to what today's feminists might expect, most of the reviews were favorable.[75] The periodicals that might have been most sympathetic to her political views defined the work relatively narrowly as a treatise on female education of which they by and large approved. The more conservative *Critical Review* saw the political arguments and significance more clearly, and disapproved more strenuously.

The traditional wisdom, that the book "was greeted with a storm of discussion, much censure, and a little discriminating praise"[76] is most likely based on the image of Wollstonecraft that developed later, as well as on Horace Walpole's famous comment that Wollstonecraft was a "hyena in petticoats." Janes points out that Walpole's observation was not in reaction to the *Rights of Woman,* which he claimed not to have read, but to Wollstonecraft's attack on Marie Antoinette in the *Rights of Men.* "As in later attacks on Wollstonecraft, Walpole's hostility was directed against the female republican writer, and not against the vindication of the rights of woman."[77]

The hatred of Wollstonecraft in some quarters began as a backwash of the storm centered on Thomas Paine (1737–1809) after the publication of his *Rights of Man*, the second edition of which was published one month after the *Rights of Woman*. Paine and Wollstonecraft were already acquaintances, and saw each other regularly later in their (1793–94) Paris days. They became linked together in the public mind as republicans, which became increasingly dangerous in England. Late in 1792 Blake warned Paine to leave the country to protect his life. In December Paine was tried and sentenced for seditious libel (i.e. *The Rights of Man*). Early the next year Eliza Wollstonecraft wrote to her sister that Paine had been burnt in effigy at Pembroke, and there was "talk of immortalizing Miss W in the same manner."[78] She was immortalized in another, related way. In 1799 when the republican artist James Barry (1741–1806) was expelled from the Royal Academy of Arts, part of the rationale was:

> That this being a Royal Academy it was sufficient ground for suspension or removal to prove that a Member avowed democratical opinions,—which Barry had done saying a *Republic* was the proper Government for Art to flourish under,—that he has highly commended *David*, & Mrs. Wolstencraft [sic] & commended their principles.[79]

Because Paine became the symbol of the treasonous Jacobin, the writer in the *Anti-Jacobin Review and Magazine* was probably not the only person to reduce Wollstonecraft by saying, "Her doctrines are almost all obvious corollaries from the theorems of Paine."[80]

At the same time, it is neither possible nor appropriate to disentangle completely the female republican from the vindicator of the rights of women. Wollstonecraft remained in the public light, thus enabling others to attack her as a republican, because she was the author of the *Vindication of the Rights of Woman*. Although the immediate reviews of this particular book were good, the tide was already turning against the radicals. On the anniversary of the fall of the Bastille the previous year a "Church and King" mob sacked the meeting places of the Dissenters as well as Joseph Priestley's house, complete with his library, scientific laboratory, and papers. The authorities did not notice the violence.

In May 1792 King George issued a Proclamation for Preventing Seditious Meetings and Writings that attacked "divers wicked and seditious writings" (no names were mentioned) "tending to scite tumult and disorder, by endeavouring to raise groundless jealousies and discontents in the minds of our faithful and loving subjects, respecting the laws and constitution of government, civil and religious." Magistrates were ordered to watch "in order to discover the authors and printers of such wicked and seditious writings." Special efforts were directed at Paine.

Efforts to suppress the radicals were extremely popular. The conservative sentiment was not simply a superficial reaction following mass support for the French Revolution.[81] Paine, Wollstonecraft, and their circle represented a small slice of English society. The legal apparatus squeezed the radicals more through the next years. The treason trial of Thomas Holcroft, John Horne Tooke, and others took place in 1794, the same year that habeas corpus was suspended. The Two Acts of November 1795 included the Treasonable and Seditious Practices Act and the Seditious Meetings Act. Joseph Johnson was eventually convicted and served time in prison.

The political culture and public opinion of the late eighteenth century has often been seriously misrepresented, so much so that it becomes difficult to understand the significance of those who persisted in liberal political speech and writing. In recent years the *Rights of Woman* has been reinterpreted and diminished by some writers as almost a minor amendment to popular views.[82] To argue that "When the rights of men were being widely proclaimed, it did not seem so extravagant to extend those rights to women"[83] is to do a serious injustice to those who historically sought justice.

The *Vindication of the Rights of Woman* was widely read during Wollstonecraft's life but was not reprinted until the middle of the nineteenth century. More than a half-century later, in 1855, George Eliot could write, "There is in some quarters a vague prejudice against the *Rights of Woman* as in some way or other a reprehensible book, but readers who go to it with this impression will be surprised to find it eminently serious, severely moral, and withal rather heavy—the true reason, perhaps, that no edition has been published since 1796." Eliot found the book wise, but entirely too rational: "she has no erudition, and her grave pages are lit up by no ray of fancy."[84] Perhaps Eliot's expectations about the wild feminist chastened her perceptions.

The *Vindication of the Rights of Woman* was not intended to be Wollstonecraft's final word on the subject. She wrote, "When I began to write this work, I divided it into three parts, supposing that one volume would contain a full discussion of the arguments which seemed to me to rise naturally from a few simple principles; but fresh illustrations occurring as I advanced, I now present only the first part to the public." She thought that "many subjects . . . which I have cursorily alluded to, call for particular investigation, especially the laws relative to women, and the consideration of their peculiar duties. These will furnish ample matter for a second volume . . ." (*VW* 70). Throughout this "first" volume she dropped hints about problems she intended to pursue further at a later date. She restated her intention to discuss law, especially marital law (*VW* 215). She also noted, "My observations on national education are obviously hints" (*VW* 242, 245). She left a series of notes to herself (which Godwin published as "Hints") about her future work on the rights of woman, but most seem to be either general comment on mind and sensibility and their development, or observations she had used in her last published piece, an essay on poetry. Probably the best hint we have about what more she might have written, or perhaps what is the early draft of the successor volume itself, is the fragment we have of her novel, *The Wrongs of Woman, or Maria.*

Although the *Vindication of the Rights of Woman* is usually regarded as her greatest work, it was by no means her last. Throughout the remainder of 1792 she continued her reviewing but was also taken up with personal matters, including the attempt to settle one of her brothers with a position in America and other financial matters. Wollstonecraft also had taken in a young girl to care for,[85]* although by the end of the year the child had been sent to Everina Wollstonecraft. That year was also the time during which Wollstonecraft's relationship with Henry Fuseli developed toward its unhappy end.

Although Wollstonecraft developed many friendships within the Johnson circle, she singled out Henry Fuseli (1741–1825) as an object of both admiration and affection. Wollstonecraft, Johnson, and Fuseli spent a lot of time together between the late 1780s and the end of 1792, when Wollstonecraft left for Paris.[86]* Fuseli was born in Switzerland and began his career as a Zwinglian minister but turned away from the church to devote himself to painting, political writing, and art history and criticism.

Fuseli wrote a pamphlet attacking church and government in 1763, and in 1767 published *Remarks on the Writings and Conduct of J.-J. Rousseau.* He was one of a number of artist/art theorists in the late eighteenth century who developed political theories of art framed by the ideals and goals of civic humanism. Fuseli regretted what he perceived as the tendency toward privatization of art. He believed that because art was increasingly sponsored and acquired by private individuals it would less often fulfill the functions of instilling public virtues and a sense of public identity. Instead of encouraging free participation of citizens in public expression, art would function only to support private splendor, acquisitive individualism, and therefore, corruption.[87]

Wollstonecraft's own writings at this time show an increasing influence of both Rousseau and the language of civic humanism, including constructions based in art history and criticism. One biographer saw Fuseli's influence in one of her book reviews.[88] Certainly she was already reading Rousseau—his *Émile*—before she and Fuseli became close,[89]* and the language of republicanism was one of the primary theoretical currencies in the circles in which she moved. But there is also considerable evidence that Fuseli was influential in her life. Most of her biographers have dwelt on the love she developed for Fuseli and her unsuccessful proposal for a ménage à trois in which she apparently offered to have the intellectual part of her beloved while his wife could keep the physical. In 1792 she was to have traveled to France with the Fuselis and Joseph Johnson in order for all of them to witness the Revolution for themselves, but following her rebuff by the Fuselis she departed by herself in December of that year, and did not return to England until 1795.

Revolutions and Journeys

In Paris Wollstonecraft again became part of a social circle defined in large part by politics. There were the foreigners who, like Wollstonecraft, came as admirers of the Revolution and, for the most part, stayed through the Terror and after. Among these were Tom Paine, Ruth and Joel Barlow, Maria Williams, and Thomas Christie. She found most of her French friends among the Girondins, including the author Stéphanie-Félicité Brulart de Genlis (Madame Genlis, 1747–1830) Manon Roland (1754–93), and Jean-Pierre Brissot (1754–93).

Soon after Wollstonecraft arrived in Paris she began a "Letter on the Present Character of the French Nation." Perhaps this was intended as another and more analytical follow-up to her response to Edmund Burke, but all that exists of it is an introductory letter dated 15 February 1793, devoted in large part to the problems social observation, particularly in the conditions then extant in Paris. It is also the first glimpse we have of the political idealist (an English Jacobin) seriously grappling with the reality of human political behavior: the Terror.

Wollstonecraft seems to have begun but never completed a report on education for the French committee on public instruction. Jean Antoine de Condorcet (1743–94), who shared many views with Wollstonecraft, was on that committee, but her contact was more likely her friend Tom Paine, also on the committee.[90]*